THE MYSTERY
OF THE TWO CHURCHES

THE MYSTERY

OF THE TWO CHURCHES

The Church That Jesus Built
And The Church That Satan Built

BOLA OLU-JORDAN

CRYOUT

The Mystery of the Two Churches:
The Church that Jesus Built and the Church that Satan Built

ISBN-10: 9785037770
ISBN-13: 978-9785037777

The Mystery of the Two Churches: the Church that Jesus Built and the Church that Satan Built and other CRYOUT Publishing books can be purchased in bulk by churches, ministries and other organizations for evangelical, educational or discipleship purposes. For information, please send your request via email to info@cryoutpublishing.com

First Printing, 2016

Printed in the United States of America.

To the Philadelphia Church

Table of Contents

Preface vii

Introduction.. ix

    CHAPTER 1: The Prophetic Church 1

    CHAPTER 2: The Mystery of the Woman 5

    CHAPTER 3: The Ministry of the Two Women ... 35

    CHAPTER 4: The Two Experiences....................... 49

    CHAPTER 5: The Characteristics of the two
                 Churches:... 53

    CHAPTER 6: The Kingdom and the Glory........... 67

Final Words 73

That he might present it to himself a glorious church, not having spot, or wrinkle, or any such thing; but that it should be holy and without blemish.
- Eph 5:27

And upon her forehead was a name written,
MYSTERY, BABYLON THE GREAT,
THE MOTHER OF HARLOTS
AND ABOMINATIONS
OF THE EARTH.
- Rev 17:5

Preface

I was working on the book, *Companion Booklet to the Normal Christian Cycle* when the revelation of this book kind of "popped up" in my heart. The flow was like a tidal wave and the tone sounded so urgent that I temporarily abandoned the other book to give this the attention I felt the Lord wanted it to have.

I tried to downplay the title, particularly the sub-title because I considered the tone a bit strong, but I was further convinced it is from the Lord when I shared the revelation with a friend and he brought out his writing pad with the same sub-title - verbatim! Since the message is a direct revelation from the Lord, the book was completed in just a few days. The weeks following was just to prepare it for final publishing.

I felt the Lord gave this message because, in recent times, I have been concerned at the stage of the last day Church (just like Lot was in Sodom). I have been burdened that the Church is failing and derailing; and also that the voices of the "whistle-blowers," the prophets are fading away, materialism is overruning the Church, and so Jesus may not meet the chaste Bride He died for. If you are also in this category, I believe the Lord's message in this book will encourage and comfort you just as it did for me.

Many thanks to brother Dennis Kekemeke and my son, Richard for doing such a wonderful editorial work on this book in such a short window of time.

Have a blessed time reading.

Introduction

For we wrestle not against flesh and blood, but against principalities, against powers, against the rulers of the darkness of this world, against spiritual wickedness in high places.
Eph 6:12

THE PASSAGE ABOVE describes the primordial and on-going battle between the kingdom of God and that of Satan. Although in effect, Satan is a created being and cannot *fight* with God as it were (Rom 9:20-21), but as in all situations, God is being glorified in the wonders of His own works, "according to His good pleasure which he hath purposed in himself," "that in all things he might have the pre-eminence," and that He "may be all in all" (Col 1:18, 1Cor 15:28).

In this struggle, however, victory is already determined before the world began, and so for those in the Kingdom of God, the fight is from victory and not for victory.

Every great king and ruler desire to have a prince to perpetuate his glory and kingdom. Same with God: He desires that His Son would rule and perpetuate the reign, glory, and majesty of His kingdom on earth just as He does in heaven. So, He created Adam and put him in the Garden of Eden to carry out this assignment.

But before this, Satan had been sent out of heaven to the earth along with a third of the angels after he led the rebellion against God with his five "I wills" (Isa 14:12-14, Luk 10:18). Since then, he colonized the earth and appropriated it as his own. He became the "prince of this world" (Joh 12:31, 14:30), "the prince of the power of the air" (Eph 2:2) -Beelzebub, "the Lord of the flies" (Luk 11:15-19)- the god of the atmospheric heavens, "the chief of the devils" and the "Lord of the devils" (Mar 3:22). He ruled and patrolled the earth "to and fro" (Job 2:2) with his angels until suddenly, Adam showed up in the Garden.

Since Satan thought the earth belonged to him, he saw Adam's presence in the Garden as an intrusion and invasion of his privacy and personal property. He took it as an assault to rob him of what is legally his, and a ploy to dethrone him of his reign on earth, which to him was the only place he could be. Little did he realize that "the earth belongs to the Lord and the fullness thereof" (Psa 24:1), just like the "heavens and the heaven of heavens" belong to Him (Deut 10:14, 1Kin 8:27). This was one pill too many for Satan to swallow, he determined not to relinquish his reign on the earth to God's Son, or accept another defeat; he would rather dislodge Him so that he could firm up his grip on his ownership over the earth. But God already equipped His Son with all that is needed to defeat him, so that as He defeated Satan in heaven, His Son also would defeat him on earth.

Suddenly, Satan struck. He unleashed a cunningly devised and carefully masterminded assault against Adam through Eve, the bride of Adam, knowing her all-important role in achieving God's mandate. With this, he "successfully" truncated the rule and reign of Adam and "stole" the earth from him. From then on, he usurped the place and position of the Son of God and ruled the earth.

However, his victory was cut short four thousand years later when the second Adam (Christ) showed up on the scene with yet another bride with whom He would take over the earth; to rule and reign in it as His Father had ordained before the foundation of the world. This time, the Son, along with the bride would finally bruise Satan's head and send him to where he rightly belongs, the lake of fire (Rev 201:10).

This battle intensifies as the end of the age closes in. Satan knows that he has only a short time, and so he is engaged in an escalated battle of his soul and the soul of the earth. He is fighting tooth and nail and leaving no stone unturned to resist God's rule and authority on earth through His Son and His bride. He wants to retain what he thinks belongs to him at all cost. He is employing the same strategy and instrument he used before, i.e. the woman, the bride of the first (and second) Adam, "the mystery of God, and of the Father, and of Christ" (Col 2:2, 4:3, Eph 3:4).

At the end, Christ will reign and "deliver up the kingdom to God, even the Father; when he shall have put down all rule and all authority and power. For he must reign, till he hath put all enemies under his feet... And when all things shall be subdued unto him, then shall the Son also himself be subject unto him that put all things under him, that God may be all in all." (1Cor 15:28)

Since God will judge the world and all things by Christ and His bride (Act 17: 31, Rom 2:16), Christ's victory and reign will not be complete without His bride by His side (1Cor 6:2). This is why Christ went to the Cross to die for her and will come back for her so that they can both reign together in victory (Eph 5:25, Joh 14:1-3). The Church (the bride) is God's barometer for Christ's victory, hence, Christ must build His Church.

For Satan to effectively counter and contend with Christ's victory, he must also have a bride, because she is the yardstick by which God measures victory (as it was in the Garden, so it is even now). So, as Jesus is committed to building His bride (the Church), Satan also is committed to building his own bride, too.

This book is written as a wake-up call to the sleeping bride, particularly, believers stranded in the organized church system. The reality of this epic struggle between [the second] Adam and Satan, and their common 'instrument,' the woman (the bride), is a call to battle, and we are a part of the warfare. The Bible calls these two brides "mysteries," and these are the two churches: one built by Jesus (through His called-out ones) and the other built by Satan, (through His ministers who transform as angels of light). You belong to one!

CHAPTER 1
The Prophetic Church

WOMAN IS THE prophetic representation of the Church (Eph 5:27), and the Church is the prophetic representation of The Bride of Christ (Rev 21:9).

The plan of God is to have His Son rule the earth just as He, the Father rules heaven. The Son must have a bride who, together in unity (just as the Trinity in heaven, Gen 1:26, 1Joh 5:7) would fulfill this mandate on earth (Gen 1:22, 2:18). God activated this plan when He presented Eve, the first woman to Adam (Gen 2:21, 3:20). She became the bride of the 'first Adam.' She also represents the prophetic bride of Christ, the second Adam. This bride is known as the Church of Jesus Christ today (Eph 5:27, 1Cor 15:45).

However, Satan truncated this plan of God by deceiving Adam's bride (Gen 3:1). He corrupted her and changed her pedigree from "without spot, stain, wrinkle, blemish or any such thing," to a fallen state of nakedness, sorrow, and shame (Gen 3:7-19). The woman thus became an "unworthy bride" for Adam to present to the Father and to fulfill the mandate to rule the earth and have dominion over it (1Tim 2:14, Gen 1:28). To forestall any immediate back-up plan of another bride for Adam by God, Satan lured the woman to also corrupt Adam himself by making him to participate in the corruption (Gen 3:6, 1Tim 2:14), and thus, both the man and the woman were deceived and under the curse and judgment, and could not fulfil God's plan (Gen 3:16-19).

Having made such a remarkable "success" in truncating the plan of God in Eden, and knowing that God had promised yet another Son who would bruise his head (Gen 3:15), and whom he would not be able to overcome as he overcame the first Adam and that the Son would ultimately have a virgin bride that is chaste, without spot, stain, wrinkle, and blemish or any such thing, Satan went ahead to make counter plans in order to maintain his "success:"

- He would deceive and corrupt the second bride so that she will no longer be pure as he did the first bride in the Garden.
- If corrupting the true bride would not work, he would persecute, afflict and if possible, kill her

and present his own counterfeit bride as a substitute.

- He created a counterfeit bride so that even if "the second Adam," Christ made it, He would only have a counterfeit bride to present to the Father, whom the Father would reject, thereby stifling the plan still.

Satan was committed to these plans and still is. The bride he created is alive and active today. She is a replica of the true bride and even goes by her name, "Church." She also possesses everything the true bride possesses with so much resemblance that if it were possible, the "very elect" would be deceived (Mat 24:24).

CHAPTER 2

The Mystery of the Woman

THE WOMAN IS the seal of the plan of God - and also of the devil, as reflected in the Garden, hence, the battle for her soul. She is the key to man's success, the perfection of the earth and the completion of man's call and assignment. Without a woman, man cannot fulfill purpose on earth.

The Bible says:

> ...And the LORD God said, It is not good that the man should be alone; I will make him an help meet for him. (Gen 2:18)

The world says:

> Behind every successful man, there is a woman.

She is a mystery (Eph 5:27), the enigma of God. The successes and respects of any man are measured by her. The writer of the book of Proverbs says, "A [virtuous] woman is a crown to her husband" (Prov. 12:4). She is the fulfillment of purposes, a game-changer in the eternal scheme and a mighty tool in the hands of the heavenly powers. She is the summation and consummation of everything sublime, but when corrupted, she is the direct opposite, a personification of evil. She may truly be a "weaker vessel" and delicate in the physical but she is mighty in the spiritual realm. This explains why Satan has never and would never leave a woman alone.

The arrival of Eve in the Garden was a sure signal that Adam was truly ready to fulfill destiny. He was ready to rule the earth which Satan thought was his by right since he was sent down from heaven (Isa 14:12). He moved in swiftly and unleashed his subtle arsenal against the innocent bride by getting her fascinated in the discovery of a 'new knowledge,' the tremendous innate ability she possessed, and that she was more powerful and beautiful than she thought (Gen 3). Alas! Eve became a victim of Satan's resistance and struggle to retain the world. She was subsequently brought down from her glorious and lofty height before she realized it. She lost the spiritual ability she possessed as a "help-mate" beside Adam and lost her place in destiny.

The Battle Continues

Many a woman have lost their position today to the same whims, caprices, and great deception of the devil. His secret weapon against women is still the deceit of what she can do, and particularly, that she is equal to man and she can do (better) what a man can do. This (evil) doctrine has crept into many Christian gatherings and celebrated right from the pulpit. Some women have taken over the pulpit, neglecting their noble role and calling. If a woman can do what a man can do then she is not necessary. She was created to do what a man cannot do and those things are many. That's why God said in the book of Genesis that, *"It is not good that the man should be alone; I will make him an help meet for him." (Gen 2:18)*

The woman is the completion of the man. She is the key to his destiny. God specially created her and endowed her with what is lacking in man and which he needs to be able succeed. That is the essence and the reason of her creation.

The doctrine of *women liberation* and *equality with men* is the greatest evil, deceit, and wickedness that ever happened to womanhood with the root from Eden. It's not a promotion, but a demotion to woman and a downgrade of her moral, social, and spiritual worth, but sadly, she does not know it. Eve believed

Satan's lies, and many still do and are busy trying to align with the commercial orchestration and promotion of the dastardly doctrine by the world, under the hidden sponsorship of Satan.

From the time Satan unleashed this great deceit on the first woman in the Garden and she swallowed it hook, line, and sinker, Satan breathed a sigh of relief and resumed his control and grip of the earth once again (Mat 4:8-9). He would go in that "victory" till the second Adam would appear on the scene to take over the kingdom of His Father in whom He is the rightful possessor.

When the second Adam, Christ Jesus was about to be born, Satan did all he could to stop Him but failed (Mat 1:1-20, 2:7-16). Terrified at Jesus' birth, he used the "wise men" to uncover His identity so that Herod could destroy Him (Mat 2:1-12). He failed. He waited to make sure His ministry never began, or a failure from the start so that the new bride [the Church] would not be born, but he failed again (Mat 4:1-10); he watched as Jesus began His ministry in glory and power. He was more distraught that the central theme of Jesus' ministry was preaching the Kingdom (which Satan was battling to appropriate to himself). Several times in the Gospel, Jesus mentioned "the kingdom," because that was His mission on earth: to restore the "kingdom" that Satan stole in the Garden (Isa 11:6-9).

Desperate and running out of time, Satan plotted to kill Jesus and get Him out of the scene as quickly as possible before the bride showed up. He knew that the bride was key to getting the kingdom and when she shows up, the kingdom is as good as taken. Little did Satan realize that his plan to "kill" Jesus was part of the plan and agenda of God to have a bride for His Son.

Eve did not arrive until Adam was "killed" (God caused him to have a 'deep sleep' - Gen 2:21). The Church also would not be birthed until Christ was "killed" (Christ's 'deep sleep,' - crucified and buried in the tomb). That is why several times Jesus was constantly saying it was important for Him to die and then rise again (Mat 12:40). His "death" is the birth of the bride and His resurrection is the rising up of the Church just like Adam's rising was the birth of Eve.

And the LORD God caused a deep sleep to fall upon Adam, and he slept: and he took one of his ribs, and closed up the flesh instead thereof; And the rib, which the LORD God had taken from man, made he a woman, and brought her unto the man. And Adam said, This is now bone of my bones, and flesh of my flesh: she shall be called Woman, because she was taken out of Man. (Gen 2:21 -23)

When Jesus rose after three days in the tomb (what a deep sleep!), God pulled out another "Eve" from Christ's [riven] side, just as He did at the beginning in Eden with Adam, and behold, the bride of Christ, the Church of the living God was born. As Adam was the head and Eve was the body, so also Christ is the head and the new bride, [the Church) is the body:

> *Now ye are the body of Christ, and members in particular. (1Cor 12:27)*

> *So we, being many, are one body in Christ, and every one members one of another. (Rom 12:5)*

> *For the husband is the head of the wife, even as Christ is the head of the church: and he is the saviour of the body. Therefore as the church is subject unto Christ, so let the wives be to their own husbands in every thing. ... For we are members of his body, of his flesh, and of his bones. For this cause shall a man leave his father and mother, and shall be joined unto his wife, and they two shall be one flesh. This is a great mystery: but I speak concerning Christ and the church. (Eph 5:23-25, 30-33)*

Who the woman was in Eden is who she is at Calvary: the mystery of God. God's promise in Eden came to pass: "I will put enmity between thee and the woman, and between thy seed and her seed; it shall bruise thy head, and thou shalt bruise his heel" (Gen 3:15). He truly bruised His heel but Christ bruised his head forever! As Eve's arrival in Eden caught Satan unawares, so also did the Church's emergence.

The Church was hidden to Satan (a mystery) just as it was hidden from the prophets (only Joel saw a glimpse of it's glorious beginning, Joel 2:28). Paul said the Church is a "mystery, which was kept secret since the world began." (Rom 16:25) Paul called the revealing of the mystery of the Church his "gospel" (Rom 2:16, 16:25, 2Tim 2:8) and that he was called "to make all men see what is the fellowship of the mystery, which from the beginning of the world hath been hid in God, who created all things by Jesus Christ." (Eph 3:9) He called it "a great mystery," speaking of Christ and the Church (Eph 5:32).

Now to him that is of power to stablish you according to my gospel, and the preaching of Jesus Christ, according to the revelation of the mystery, which was kept secret since the world began. (Rom 16:25)

The rest of the apostles also acknowledged the fact that the mystery of the Church is the "wisdom of God" as revealed to Paul (2Pet 3:15).

How could Satan have known that killing Jesus Christ would be his undoing to bringing forth the woman he feared most! He lost, but then, he restrategized: his focus from then on shifted to the bride (the Church), who was born right in his nose and he was helpless because Christ is doing a sure work.

Satan reverted to his old strategy: to corrupt the bride (the Church) so that she would no longer be a virgin and no longer qualify as the bride of Christ, and Christ would have no pure bride to come back to. He also created his own bride, also a mystery woman called, "the mystery babylon:"

> *... the great whore that sitteth upon many waters: With whom the kings of the earth have committed fornication, and the inhabitants of the earth have been made drunk with the wine of her fornication... a woman sit upon a scarlet coloured beast, full of names of blasphemy, having seven heads and ten horns. And the woman was arrayed in purple and scarlet colour, and decked with gold and precious stones and pearls, having a golden cup in her hand full of abominations and filthiness of her fornication: And upon her forehead was a name written, MYSTERY, BABYLON THE GREAT, THE*

MOTHER OF HARLOTS AND ABOMI-NATIONS OF THE EARTH... the woman drunken with the blood of the saints, and with the blood of the martyrs of Jesus: and when I saw her, I wondered with great admiration. (Rev 17:1-6)

This is the counterfeit bride Satan created to use for his own purposes to counter the plan of God for Christ. She is a harlot, not the virgin without stain, spot, or wrinkle or any such thing like the bride of Christ. She is "the abomination of all the earth" (Rev 17:5), and have offsprings who are also harlots fostering the same assignment.

The Two Women Compared

This is the comparison of the two women:

1. **The Counterfeit Bride.** A harlot and mother of all harlots (Rev 17:5). She shares her abominations with her offspring who are also harlots (Rev 14:18, 16:19, 17:4-6), "the abomination of the earth." Her power is deception. She is so mysterious that she "…made all nations drink of the wine of the wrath of her fornication." She is the false and counterfeit church.

She is also called "the strange woman." The writer of the book of Proverbs says, she flatters with her words; …forsakes guide of her youth, and forgets the covenant of her God…None that go unto her return again, neither take they hold of the paths of life (Prov 2:16-19).

Her ministry is reflected today in many sugar-coated messages by preachers who speak "great swelling words of vanity," sweet messages that scintillate people's ears, fables, lies from the pulpit (2Tim 4:3-4, 1Cor 2:1-4). They teach how to develop the innate power of the soul and ability to do the near impossible by positive thinking and confession and yet get immediate and phenomenal result. Alas! "all nations have drunk of the wine of the wrath of her fornication, and the kings of the earth have committed fornication with her, and the merchants of the earth are waxed rich through the abundance of her delicacies" (Rev 18:3).

The writer warns:

Lust not after her beauty in thine heart; neither let her take thee with her eyelids. For by means of a whorish woman a man is brought to a piece of bread: and the adulteress will hunt for the precious life." (Prov 6:24)

That they may keep thee from the strange woman, from the stranger which flattereth with her words. (Prov 7:5)

The book of Revelation described her as sitting "upon a scarlet coloured beast, full of names of blasphemy, having seven heads and ten horns" (Rev 17:3). She is represented in all nations of the earth, in every tongue, tribe and race. She is the be-all-and-end-all of her religion and her children (denominations) have lovely names, structure, system, power, money, beauty, and attractions to bring many in.

The lips of a strange woman drop as an honeycomb, and her mouth is smoother than oil: But her end is bitter as wormwood, sharp as a twoedged sword. Her feet go down to death; her steps take hold on hell. Lest thou shouldest ponder the path of life, her ways are moveable, that thou canst not know them. Hear me now therefore, O ye children, and depart not from the words of my mouth. Remove thy way far from her, and come not nigh the door of her house: Lest thou give thine honour unto others, and thy years unto the cruel. (Prov 5:3-9)

As a bride (of Satan) she is rich and uses her riches as a bait and her robe as honor and respect:

And the woman was arrayed in purple and scarlet colour, and decked with gold and precious stones and pearls, having a golden cup in her hand full of abominations and filthiness of her fornication. (Rev 17:4)

She is the arch-enemy of the true woman, she persecutes and wages war with her continuously. She desires to take her position like Hagar desired to take the position of Sarah who was the mother of the Promised child, Isaac. But according to how it is written, "Cast out this bondwoman and her son: for the son of this bondwoman shall not be heir with my son, even with Isaac." (Gen 21:10, Rev 12:13) So also this counterfeit church cannot be the bride of Christ, regardless.

Being the copy-cat that Satan is, always mimicking and counterfeiting everything of God, and running ahead with his alternative to creating a fire-work in order to circumvent the original and deceive, Satan is busy and committed to 'building his Church' with all the possible attraction. No mortal is immuned from his deception except by the Spirit of God. He is everywhere and his ministers are eloquent, brilliant, powerful, and anointed,

> ...for such are false apostles, deceitful workers, transforming themselves into the apostles of Christ. And no marvel; for Satan himself is transformed into an angel of light. Therefore it is no great thing if his ministers also be transformed as the ministers of righteousness; whose end shall be according to their works. (2Cor 11:13-15)

One of the greatest successes of his ministry is the lack of suspicion and religious acceptance. He has deceived and still deceiving the whole world, and if it were possible, will deceive "the very elect."

The True Bride (Rev 21:9). She is a glorious Church, built by Jesus Himself, without "spot, or wrinkle, or any such thing; but that it should be holy and without blemish" (Eph 5:27, Rev 21:9). She is also called "the virtuous woman (Prov 12:4, 31:10). She is the Church of Jesus Christ whom He died for, purchased with His blood and coming back for -the Bride of Christ. She is chaste, pure and undefiled (2Cor 11:12). She also has a robe:

And I John saw the holy city, new Jerusalem, coming down from God out of heaven, prepared as a bride adorned for her husband (Rev 21:2)

And to her was granted that she should be arrayed in fine linen, clean and white: for the fine linen is the righteousness of saints. (Rev 19:8)

These two women are the prophetic representation of the church: one is the counterfeit church and the other is the true Church of the remnant assembly, and both are here with us. Whose member are you of? (1Cor 1:12, 3:4, 12:12-26)

The Two Cities

These two *women* (churches) are also prophetically referred to as "cities" (Rev 14:8, 16:19, 18:10, Rev 21:2).

1. The Abominable City:

This is a city built by Satan. It is religious (not spiritual) and the counterfeit of the New Jerusalem, "the city of God." Each religion of the world is an expression of this city and Satan is the overall head and king.

And there followed another angel, saying, Babylon is fallen, is fallen, that great city, because she made all nations drink of the wine of the wrath of her fornication. (Rev 14:8)

The "city" is made by each denomination building towards the head [quarter] of their sect for religious identification and ecumenism. That was the "noble" course of Nimrod:

Go to, let us build us a city and a tower, whose top may reach unto heaven; and let us make us a name, lest we be scattered abroad upon the face of the whole earth. (Gen 11:4)

This is the beginning of Babel, denominations! Today, every religion and denominations are trying to build something exclusive for themselves. Here is what the Lord said:

And the LORD came down to see the city and the tower, which the children of men builded. And the LORD said, Behold, the people is one, and they have all one language; and this they begin to do: and now nothing will be restrained from them, which they have imagined to do. (Gen 11: 5-6)

Notice God's word, *"…nothing will be restrained from them which they IMAGINED to do."* This is the power of imagination, ingenious mind creation, and control. Man can do practically anything he imagines to do without God because he is the image and likeness of God. It will be done by soul power (positive thinking and positive confession). At the root of this is Satan, the king of the soul realm.

The ideology is the same today as different denominations strive to build mega this and mega that: churches, institutions, cathedrals, empires, or something of that magnitude to show growth, religious commitment, and activities. It is purportedly for the "glory of God and mankind" but a show of what man can do for God, which is religion, and God "hates" religion. He did not give us religion, He gave us Christ. The idea is always noble and good but not all that is good is of God. He told children of Israel to dwell in tents. He told the disciples to "carry neither purse, nor scrip, nor shoes: and salute no man by the way" (Luk 10:4).

Christianity is a call to a life of simplicity; to leave the world (the glory) and all that is in or of the world (the system -1Joh 2:15) and simply follow a Person, Jesus (Mat 4:7-8, 9:29, 19:21, Mar 10:24-28). This does not suggest a life of poverty or penury, but a life of self-denial that is not controlled by these things and not focused on them but on Christ. Ultimately, "all these things shall be added" by Christ as needed, but we must not seek after or live for them (Mat 6:32-33).

Today, many are in ministry for the gains, show, and the accolades. Many are self-sent or man-sent and carry more than a purse, scrip and shoes to fulfill their ambition of success in ministry. They are materialistic, many to a point of insanity, (or how do one explain someone with a huge congregation that people cannot approach and have many exotic cars parked in garages, purportedly for evangelism and "rural mission" in many bad roads in parts of Africa). Paul said,

(For many walk, of whom I have told you often, and now tell you even weeping, that they are the enemies of the cross of Christ: Whose end is destruction, whose God is their belly, and whose glory is in their shame, who mind earthly things.) (Php 3:18)

21

Many live in stupendous wealth gotten from deceit and promise of miracles, healing or a better life for the congregants who keep giving out of lack so they can have, and so enrich the leader who has an insatiable appetite for inanities. He builds empires and edifices inaccessible to these people and burdens himself with titles and respects only meant and next to God.

This is the same spirit in Gehazi, the servant of prophet Elisha in the Bible. Even though Elisha rejected the expensive clothes and other gifts offered to him by General Naaman as an appreciation of being healed of his leprosy through him, but his servant, Gehazi, went behind his back to collect them (2Kin 5:2-25). Elisha knew what his servant did, Jesus also knows what these so-called "men of God" are doing, and at the end, "...he shall say, I tell you, I know you not whence ye are; depart from me, all ye workers of iniquity" (Luk 13:27).

People call their wonderful structures and edifices "the Church," and their institutions and empires evidences of the power and presence of God. That was what Abraham wanted to do with Ishmael until God stopped and silenced him, and asked him to send both the child and the mother away (Gen 21:12-14). We must do away with such edifices and ministry that have become our religious pride fueled by the income generating system and mechanism brought into the New Testament Church in order to remain in business and to build personal empire rather than the Kingdom of God (Mal 3:8-12). We must learn from Paul:

Even unto this present hour we both hunger, and thirst, and are naked, and are buffeted, and have no certain dwelling place; And labour, working with our own hands: being reviled, we bless; being persecuted, we suffer it: Being defamed, we intreat: we are made as the filth of the world, and are the offscouring of all things unto this day. I write not these things to shame you, but as my beloved sons I warn you. (1Cor 4:11-14)

We are New Testament people, no more tribes of Levis or Judah, Jews or Gentiles, bond or free, but brethren; brothers and sisters, priests and kings (1Pet 2:9, Rev 5:10). "For by one Spirit are we all baptized into one body, whether we be Jews or Gentiles, whether we be bond or free; and have been all made to drink into one Spirit." (1Cor 12:13) Consequently, we can all come boldly to the throne of grace to obtain mercy in times of needs (Heb 4:6).

Paul said further,

But what things were gain to me, those I counted loss for Christ. Yea doubtless, and I count all things but loss for the excellency of the knowledge of Christ Jesus my Lord: for whom I have suffered the loss of all things, and do count them but dung, that I may win Christ, And be found in him, not having mine own righteousness, which is of the law, but that which is through the faith of Christ, the righteousness which is of God by faith: That I may know him, and the power of his resurrection, and the fellowship of his sufferings, being made conformable unto his death (Php 3:7-10)

This man wrecked havoc against the Church with his religious pride (Act 8). Later when he got the spiritual understanding, he confessed that he did it in "ignorance and unbelief" thinking he was doing God a service (1Tim 1:13). He was previously "using" God, just like many do today. God did not use him until he realized this. Imagine the further havoc this man could have done to the Church and the society if Christ did not stop him (Act 9). It can only be compared to what the descendants of Ishmael are doing to the world today. Imagine having many of that in the world!

Many have risen in history in similar spirit but stopped by God: Hitler and Napoleon are handy examples. But many Christian leaders today are still in the same spirit under a different umbrella of religion.

They are building movements, empires, institutions where one man is the head, and gather people together purportedly to lead them before God like Nimrod did. This leadership style is never the idea of God and that was what led to Babel, and today, it is still Babylon and a rebellion against God. That is why the ideal Church leadership ordained by Christ and practised by the early Church is the plurality of eldership, who all hold fast to the one head, who is Christ Himself (Act 14:23, 15:2,4,22,23, 16:4, 20:17, 1Tim 5:17, Tit 1:5, Jas 5:14, 1Pet 5:1, Col 2:19).

Remember that leadership is servanthood, it is to serve the people.

Jesus called them to him, and saith unto them, Ye know that they which are accounted to rule over the Gentiles exercise lordship over them; and their great ones exercise authority upon them. But so shall it not be among you: but whosoever will be great among you, shall be your minister: And whosoever of you will be the chiefest, shall be servant of all. (Mar 10:42-44)

God does not want "leaders" to exert lordship or authority over his people. This is "gentile" practice. They are to lead and not rule:

And he sat down, and called the twelve, and saith unto them, If any man desire to be first, the same shall be last of all, and servant of all. (Mar 9:35)

The same goes for giving undue titles to these people.

But be not ye called Rabbi: for one is your Master, even Christ; and all ye are brethren. And call no man your father upon the earth: for one is your Father, which is in heaven. Neither be ye called masters: for one is your Master, even Christ. But he that is greatest among you shall be your servant. (Mat 23:8-11)

Even though the function is true (just like in the five-fold ministry of pastor, teacher, prophet, apostle and evangelist) but must not be titled because "…all ye are brethren." (Mat 23:8) Titles bring class, hierarchy and division, and that is what brought the clergy-laity practice today in the church which was a pagan style and system of leadership and it is for exclusively for control.

The one-man leadership style cannot but always results into control, even if it is done with humility and sincerity. It is the deeds and doctrine of Nicolaitans, which Jesus said He "hates" (Rev 2: 6,15), because it is the spirit of religion.

Religious people "love the uppermost rooms at feasts, and the chief seats in the synagogues, And greetings in the markets, and to be called of men, Rabbi, Rabbi…" (Mat 23:7). Even Jesus called his disciples "friends" and "brethren" (Mat 28:10, Joh 15:15, Rom 8:29), the term used throughout the New Testament Church. Unfortunately, this is one of the practices and styles that the denominations inherited from Babylon (Catholicism). It was left undealt with even by the Reformers of the sixteenth century. It is similar to the great sin of the Old Testament Israel that no king could overcome:

…Nevertheless he cleaved unto the sins of Jeroboam the son of Nebat, which made Israel to sin; he departed not therefrom. (2Kin 3:3)

This term is very common in the Old Testament of great and godly kings who "did right in the sight of the Lord" but did not depart from the sin of Jeroboam the son of Nebat WHO MADE ISRAEL TO SIN. The sin was the golden calf that he made and offered sacrifices in the high places leading Israel to sin. (1Kin 12)

The one-man leadership is also the golden calf of the Reformation that is still sacred today. Without this, there cannot be empires built by denominational heads and overseers, and there cannot be the "great city," which is headed by the overall head to counterfeit the Holy City, the New Jerusalem, the City of God.

John saw that the "great city" was indeed a woman that actually conquered kings, nobles and all the inhabitants of the earth.

And the woman which thou sawest is that great city, which reigneth over the kings of the earth. (Rev 17:18)

She was referred to as the "great city" in the following scriptures:

Standing afar off for the fear of her torment, saying, Alas, alas, that great city Babylon, that mighty city! for in one hour is thy judgment come. (Rev 18:10)

She appears to control the world right now owing to her popularity, recognition, and followership, but she will fail, fall and her judgment, as well as that of her master will be terrible (Rev 14:8, 18:2,8).

And the great city was divided into three parts, and the cities of the nations fell: and great Babylon came in remembrance before God, to give unto her the cup of the wine of the fierceness of his wrath. (Rev 16:19)

2. The Holy City:

This is the city built by Jesus Christ according to His promise: "I will build my Church." It is a heavenly city, the New Jerusalem, "the city of God."

But ye are come unto mount Sion, and unto the city of the living God, the heavenly Jerusalem, and to an innumerable company of angels. (Heb 12:22)

This city is not made with hands, and believers are given the hope of this city:

But now they desire a better country, that is, an heavenly: wherefore God is not ashamed to be called their God: for he hath prepared for them a city. (Heb 11:6)

And hath raised us up together, and made us sit together in heavenly places in Christ Jesus. (Eph 2:6)

The city is expressed by the gathering of the "called-out ones" in assembly or fellowship (ekklesia). This is the true bride, that Jesus died for and purchased with His precious blood and He's coming back to take to His Father. It is the Church of the living God.

This glorious city also has "able ministers of the New Testament; not of the letter, but of the spirit: for the letter killeth, but the spirit giveth life." (2Cor 3:6) They are sent by the Lord Jesus with no purse, nor scrip, nor shoes. They have not corrupted or used the gift of God deceitfully, to advance personal causes or build a name, city, institution or empire after themselves. They are irrevocably committed to the love and the cause of their Lord and Master, Jesus Christ. They are those who say boldly:

> *Who shall separate us from the love of Christ? shall tribulation, or distress, or persecution, or famine, or nakedness, or peril, or sword? As it is written, For thy sake we are killed all the day long; we are accounted as sheep for the slaughter. Nay, in all these things we are more than conquerors through him that loved us. For I am persuaded, that neither death, nor life, nor angels, nor principalities, nor powers, nor things present, nor things to come, Nor height, nor depth, nor any other creature, shall be able to separate us from the love of God, which is in Christ Jesus our Lord. (Rom 8:35-39)*

As regards materialism and commercializing the gifts and calling of God in building empires for themselves, they testify:

But we had the sentence of death in ourselves, that we should not trust in ourselves, but in God which raiseth the dead. (2Cor 1:9)

They are people who have lost their lives for the gospel and count all things but loss and dung for Christ's sake.

But what things were gain to me, those I counted loss for Christ. Yea doubtless, and I count all things but loss for the excellency of the knowledge of Christ Jesus my Lord: for whom I have suffered the loss of all things, and do count them but dung, that I may win Christ, And be found in him, not having mine own righteousness, which is of the law, but that which is through the faith of Christ, the righteousness which is of God by faith: That I may know him, and the power of his resurrection, and the fellowship of his sufferings, being made conformable unto his death; If by any means I might attain unto the resurrection of the dead. (Php 3:7-11)

They are brothers among brethren, not thin gods among members. The members of the body of Christ are many, yet one body, the body of Christ, the bride of Christ, the "Holy City," the functioning, replica, and manifestation of the heavenly Jerusalem, the city of

God. The "mount Sion, ...the city of the living God, the heavenly Jerusalem..." (Heb 12:22). Jesus said:

> *Him that overcometh will I make a pillar in the temple of my God, and he shall go no more out: and I will write upon him the name of my God, and the name of the city of my God, which is new Jerusalem, which cometh down out of heaven from my God: and I will write upon him my new name. (Rev 3:12)*

> *And he carried me away in the spirit to a great and high mountain, and shewed me that great city, the holy Jerusalem, descending out of heaven from God... (Rev 21:10)*

It appears as if this woman is lost, has failed, and destitute, not having a house let alone a city. She has no popularity, she is persecuted, lonely and scanty, her husband is away with a promise to come back, but he's yet to return after over two thousand years! Yet, she keeps herself pure, undefiled, unspotted, unstained, and waiting for her husband to come take her home. Although, she is growing weary under the persecution of the counterfeit church (not even by Islam), but then, one day, her husband will come as promised, and all the sufferings and sorrows will be over and her husband shall wipe away her tears. John saw the glimpse of her glory:

And I John saw the holy city, new Jerusalem, coming down from God out of heaven, prepared as a bride adorned for her husband. (Rev 21:2)

She will take her rightful place beside her husband who bought her with His precious blood, and they will rule according to the eternal plan of God, forever and ever. (Rev 3:12, 21:2)

Paul said this woman, with her husband shall judge the world:

Do ye not know that the saints shall judge the world? ...Know ye not that we shall judge angels? how much more things that pertain to this life? (1Cor 6:2-3)

And I saw heaven opened, and behold a white horse; and he that sat upon him was called Faithful and True, and in righteousness he doth judge and make war. (Rev 19:11)

Amen, and finally, Satan lost!

CHAPTER 3

The Ministry of the Two Women

THESE TWO WOMEN (churches) have parallel ministries. The ministry of the counterfeit woman (organized church system) is to make all her children (denominations) harlots so that they can represent her and spread her harlotry all over the world. Through deception, they are to deceive the whole earth, *fornicate* with the world and make "the whole world" drunk from the cup of her abomination so that the whole earth would go after her (and not the true bride) in a religious orgy under the guise of "serving God." John said:

> *And the woman was arrayed in purple and scarlet colour, and decked with gold and precious stones and pearls, having a golden cup in her hand full of abominations and filthiness of her fornication: And upon her forehead was a name written, MYSTERY, BABYLON THE GREAT, THE MOTHER OF HARLOTS AND ABOMI-NATIONS OF THE EARTH. (Rev 17:4-6)*

As you can see, she represents wealth, royalty, and splendor, "the great whore that sitteth upon many waters." Water prophetically represent people. She is such a 'professional' harlot and deceiver that "...the kings of the earth have committed fornication, and the inhabitants of the earth have been made drunk with the wine of her fornication" (Rev 17:2).

Christianity is a common religion in many nations of the world, but it is that of the strange woman. She has represented Christianity with materialism, power, and control. She brags: "I am rich, and increased with goods, and have need of nothing..." (Rev 3:17). She is so rich that she has a whole city to herself here on earth to mimick the city of the true bride, the New Jerusalem (Rev 21:2).

Her other ministry is to destroy the virgin bride and her offspring:

And I saw the woman drunken with the blood of the SAINTS, and with the blood of the MARTYRS of Jesus: and when I saw her, I wondered with great admiration. (Rev 17:6)

She seems to be winning, looking at the magnitude of her dragnet and deception —"the whole earth." She still drinks the blood of the saints (the disciples of Jesus) and makes many (remnants) martyrs since the early Church when she usurped the authority and displaced the true Church (Luk 23:3).

She persecuted and killed many apostles, disciples, and saints through the dark ages. She clamped down on true Christians till she successfully annihilated meeting in homes, houses, and simple gatherings which is the true model of the true Church (assembly) as practiced by the early Church.

Since the Emperor of Rome made the decree that 'Christianized' all citizens and made Christianity a state religion in the then Roman empire, all religions, including the worshippers of Baal became "Christians" by default. Assembly in homes was replaced with meeting in civic and public buildings in order to accommodate EVERYONE in the now UNIVERSAL Church. That is where the word "Catholic" came from, meaning "universal," or "everyone." These worshippers of Baal later became the principal officers in the *new church*. They shared positions and replaced their priestly roles in the former religion with the "five-fold ministry" of pastors, prophets, bishops, evangelists, and apostles, turning it from functions to titles, and continued their pagan practices and rituals as "Christians." Many of their practices, beliefs, festivals, names, etc, were adopted and assimilated to the new Christianity. Their idol of "queen of heaven" and the mother of their (sun) god became Mary, the "mother of God" and the (sun) god became Jesus, the son of God, giving way to the worship of the sun-god (mother and child). The celebration of the goddess "Ishtar" became "Easter." Christmas also, a pagan festival of the birth of the sun-god was celebrated as the birth of Jesus. All these were done under the *new Christian Church* in continuation of their pagan worship to the embarrassment and bewilderment of the brethren and the early Church who were powerless against the emperor's decree.

These new church officers gained influence, power, positions, and popularity. They started to persecute the saints and the true Church who would not participate in the day light robbery. By the Middle Ages, these officers, with the instrument of the state had successfully annihilated all the blue-print and template of the early Church. The pattern, model of worship, and meeting were destroyed and prohibited. It became an offense punishable by death to have a "bible" or meet in homes. The priests of Baal introduced their own doctrines, practices, and styles (like infant baptism, indulgences, clergy-laity, worship of Mary, etc). They translated the "Bible" to reflect their doctrines and destroyed the original scrolls, killing everyone who had any. They also destroyed thousands of the caves where the scrolls were kept.

This period in history is called "the dark ages." The "Universal Church" clamped down on true believers and introduced the universal "confession of faith" in order to fish out hidden believers because they would not recite it.

By and by, this Universal Church became so powerful that they also took over the control of the state. The leader of the church became the leader of the empire and was called the supreme one, "Pontifex Maximus," literarily translated "the great high priest," the Pope and appointed for life. The caption on his cap reads *"Vicarius filli dei,"* which is translated "in the place of God." Many have interpreted the Roman numerals of that word to be "666." He was vested with (and still is) the power to forgive or retain sin, pronounce death or sainthood on anyone as he pleased. He is represented, honored, respected in the whole world and recognized as the overall head of the Christian Church, but it is the "Universal Church," not the true Church. When you know the history, you will agree with those who say that Islam is closer to Christianity than Catholicism.

Truly, the "whole world" has gone after this counterfeit. Sadly, the Bible says she has been given power to "make war with the saints, and to overcome them: and power was given him over all kindreds, and tongues, and nations" (Rev 13:7).

Somehow, the true Church survived the persecution and annihilation of the dark ages. This is due majorly to the fact that Christ Himself is irrevocably committed to having a bride and a remnant for Himself that the gates of hell would not prevail against, otherwise, the true church would have died, just like Christianity "died" in Turkey, which used to be a predominantly Christian country (all the "Seven Churches of Asia" were located there) but today, it is a 98% Muslim country.

The remnant Church is still unknown, unsung, and unattractive because it is the true Church and shares the characteristic of the truth: the truth is always bitter, hated, and unwanted. Paul said, "we are made as the filth of the world, and are the offscouring of all things unto this day" (1Cor 4:13). She is still being persecuted by the Universal Church because she has remained chaste, pure, without spot or blemish. She will not compromise or participate in the mere fanfare, social, and commercial Christianity the counterfeit church is enmeshed in, which she is using to deceive and to make the whole earth follow her. Her deception is "wine"- something sweet: music, accommodative gospel, fables, sweet talk and sugar-coated messages, miracles, signs and wonders, empire building, non-spiritual matter, money, power, fame, prosperity, festivals, etc "...she made ALL NATIONS drink of the wine ..." (Rev 14:8).

The counterfeit *woman* (church) has perfected her plans and deceptions over many millennia so much so that she laces it with these irresistible religious practices. She is not hiding, she is in full glare; popular, relevant, recognized, and enjoys patronage. She is being praised, worshiped and exalted every day by sincere and innocent people who have been deceived. They think they are worshipping Christ but are indeed worshipping "the man of sin... who opposes and exalts himself "above all that is called God, or that is worshiped; so that he as God sitteth in the temple of God, shewing himself that he is God" (2The 2:4).

The persecution of the dark ages was so great that at the end it was said that no true Christian existed again. The counterfeit church was happily championing the execution of the saints, giving them a false identity before the populace and reasons why they had to be killed just as they did to Jesus (Mat 26:59). They fed many saints to wild animals at the Coliseum to the clapping spectators and relaxation of governors, dignitaries, and other Christians who have been equally brainwashed. These are just a part of the many untold, inhumane, and unimaginable death meted to the saints by the so-called "church"who grew in titles, hierarchy, costumes, etc. They burned many others at the stake whom they labeled "heretics". It was a great sacrifice and offering to their god. The saints in the true Church fled to escape the growing persecution and were scattered abroad.

With all oppositions crushed, the counterfeit Church consolidated her overthrow, took total and final control and existed as "the Church" for several hundred years following. In the early sixteenth century, however, some individuals, led by Martin Luther and continued by John Calvin, Zwingli and others actively challenged the Papal authority and the Catholic Church's doctrines, power, and many of the practices. This led to the Reformation which later broke the church into fragments and factions known as denominations today.

Even though many denominations today do not have a formal or direct dealing or affiliation with the Church of Rome or England again and are independent, they are still the offspring of the great Babylon, the offshoot of Catholicism and her seed (of harlotry) is in them. They still romance many of her practices in meetings, prayers, ministry, clergy, etc. Doing away with them would destroy the foundation such doctrines are built which have existed for several hundred years. That is why it is difficult for denominations to have true fellowship because the foundation of true fellowship (as brethren in the early church's style) was destroyed to give way to the clergy-laity (priest-people) style which is the pattern of the Baal worship and a pyramidal system of leadership, which makes one person the head or the ruler of the whole bunch and others carrying the one man.

The counterfeit church today is no longer known by her ancient name of "Babylon" or religious names of "Catholic" (universal) church but by many modern, choice, and beautiful names. They are still the greatest opposition to the true Church in practice as she continues to lure her away with ingenious attractions, soulical appeal, materialism, viral presence, and "…great signs and wonders; insomuch that, if *it were* possible, they shall deceive the very elect. Behold, I have told you before" (Mat 24:34-25). They have "a form of godliness, but denying the power thereof: from such turn away." (2Tim 3:5)

The only way out is not to try to "reform" or "protest" against her but to exit the system. God only changes people, not system, and He has not called us to change any system but our own ways. He is the only one who can do that. "And I heard another voice from heaven, saying, "Come out of her, my people, that ye be not partakers of her sins, and that ye receive not of her plagues." (Rev 18:4).

So, we see that the greatest opposition to the Church is not Islam per se but the (counterfeit) church herself, recognized by the state and accepted by the world. Jesus did not under-estimate her powers, He said, "…for the elect's sake those days shall be shortened." (Mat 24:22). What this means is that if the days were not shortened (by God), the true Church would not be able to stand her deception, just like Eve could not. Consequently, there would be no bride for the second Adam, i.e., no saints would be alive to be raptured, "but for the elect's sake…" (Mat 24:24)

Just as God moved to salvage Adam and Eve after the fall, "lest they ate from the tree of life and live forever" (Gen 3:2), so also would He move swiftly to save the remnant, otherwise, no saint will escape the mastery, and no bride for Jesus to present to the Father in order to fulfil His mission on earth.

Why is this so? Because the deceit is laced in religion, and Satan is the god of all religions, including the Christian religion. Religion is the best-selling product of Satan to the world, and Christianity is a preferred brand. It is using the name of (false) Christ to deceive the people of Christ. This world is yet to recover and may not recover from the religious deception.

Many saints are victims right now. They are trapped and stranded with the counterfeit woman and her harlot offspring (the organized church system). The world is held spellbound and deceived by the miracles, wonders, fame, power, and wealth of the offspring of the woman being perpetuated using the name of Jesus. The world is captivated by the fanfare, organization, socio-religious activities in the organized church system compared to the simplicity of true Christianity.

The Jesus of the organized church system is the Jesus of material success, fame, power, money, etc. He is not the Jesus that was crucified in Golgotha. He is not the Jesus that is busy to have a pure virgin in righteousness as a bride to present to the Father in other to fulfill His Father's will. The organized church system has deregulated the mission of Jesus to mere breakthrough, miracles, good life, and so on. The Spirit in the organized church system is the spirit of the world, not the Spirit of Christ. The gospel being preached is the gospel of materials. Paul expressed his fear saying,

But I fear, lest by any means, as the serpent beguiled Eve through his subtilty, so your minds

should be corrupted from the simplicity that is in Christ. For if he that cometh preacheth another Jesus, whom we have not preached, or if ye receive another spirit, which ye have not received, or another gospel, which ye have not accepted, ye might well bear with him. (2Cor 11:3-14)

But again, as God always have a remnant for himself in all ages, He has a remnant for Himself at the last days, the true bride, known only to her Lord and Master who is coming back to take her out of the corruption of the world "that he might present it to himself a glorious Church, not having spot, or wrinkle, or any such thing; but that it should be holy and without blemish" (Eph 5:27) .

There is only a one-way ticket to escape the mastery of the mystery woman (the organized church system): "Come out of her, my people, that ye be not partakers of her sins, and that ye receive not of her plagues." (Rev 18:4) Paul warned:

Be ye not unequally yoked together with un-believers: for what fellowship hath righteousness with unrighteousness? and what communion hath light with darkness? And what concord hath Christ with Belial? or what part hath he that believeth with an infidel? And what agreement hath the temple of God with idols? for ye are the temple of the living God; as God hath said, I will dwell in them, and walk in them; and I will be their God, and they shall be my people. Wherefore come out from among them, and be ye separate, saith the Lord, and touch not the unclean thing; and I will receive you, And will be a Father unto you, and ye shall be my sons and daughters, saith the Lord Almighty. (2Cor 6:14-18)

CHAPTER 4
The Two Experiences

THE TWO ICONIC entities (brides) are parallel lines with a world of difference in structure, message, ministry, doctrine, the way of life, and hope. However, the counterfeit Church has formulated a pseudo experience to deceive even the true seeker. It takes the Holy Spirit to reveal the fine line of demarcation separating the two experiences.

The true Church is experienced:

1. In God (Joh 17:3, 1The 1:9).
2. Through Jesus (Phi 3:8-10, Gal 2:20, Col 2:6-8, Eph 1:17, 3:19).
3. By the Holy Spirit (Joh 14:26, Joh 16:13).

The experience of God in the true Church is by the Spirit and in the Spirit because the Church is a "spiritual house" (1Pet 2:5). The Holy Spirit makes us to experience Him in our [new] "inner-man" (Joh 4:10, 2Cor 4:16, Eph 4:23, Col 3:10). He also brings us to a knowing, a revelation of God and our sonship in

Him. This is not derived through intellect or any other good but humanly devised knowledge of knowing God, particularly, theology but through the witness within (Rom 8:16).

Our services and worship also are a spontaneous response to the discovery of God, His works, power, and majesty impressed in our hearts by His Spirit, and which flows out in songs, praise, or other forms of expression to glorify Him. It is only what comes from God into our hearts that can flow back to Him in acceptable worship (Act 17:28, Phi 2:13). We are the primary sacrifice He desires, not any of our offerings (Rom 12:1). This is often a place and time of brokenness and sobriety which the solemn presence of God always brings (1Kg 19:11-12). This is a direct negation of the other experience which energizes the flesh and brings it to an orgy, soulical excitement or religious exuberance, and with cultural or traditional embellishment resulting in loud and gibberish motions which are of the flesh.

The true experience of God is by faith alone through the grace of God alone, not works or activities (Eph 2:8). The working of God in our hearts is from in to out, not out to in (Rom 4:4). It is by waiting on God and trusting His direction to lead (Act 2:1-5). Although faith is abstract and invisible, it has

EVIDENCE and SUBSTANCE (Heb 11:1), so also is the Church of Jesus; it is invisible and cannot be touched or seen but expressed in ecclesia (substance and evidence) by a remnant assembly in a gathering of saints (Rom 16:5, Rom 11:5, Heb 12:23).

However, the counterfeit Church is experienced through:

1. Christian religion.
2. Denominations (1Cor 1:10-13, Joh 17:22).
3. Works and religious activities (Luk 10:38-42, Gal 1:6-9, 1Cor 13:1-3, Col 2:20-23).

The experience is mostly soulical and often through the faculty of the mind, reasons, will, intellect, and emotions. Everything is about the soul and mental accent orchestrated by systemic or religious order. It is performance-based and energized by works, creeds, systems, laws, and codes. It is often guided or prescribed by the constituted head to compensate for the lack of the inner flow or witness of the Spirit. Leading is by the desire of the soul and the cravings of the flesh (Eph 2:3).

The worship, service, and other religious devotion is often guided or coordinated to fit an approved pattern of the constituted council or approved presbytery and appeal to the minds of the participants and congregations so as to keep them as members. It is geared towards a sensual feeling, a religious experience, or display of emotions. To them, these are manifestations and evidence of the presence of the Spirit of God.

This type of experience is common and can be seen in places where worship, programs and other beautiful and appealing activities, including soul winning, etc are carried out. It gives a sense of religious fulfillment as laid down rules are adhered to. All activities are patterned and structured exclusively to a denomination. Membership is by joining. Performance is measured by obeying rules, commitment to the leadership and show of religious conviction is the qualification for being called a 'Christian' (2Tim 3:5) without necessarily having a personal experience of Christ or the spiritual birth which is the first of several stages of the Christian life and living (Col 2:6-7, 2Pet 1:10, Heb 5:4).

The two experiences described above look very similar in practice but parallel in principles and applications. They define the two churches: one built by Jesus - spiritual (Mat 16:18, 1Pet 2:5, Eph 5:27), the true Church, energized by the Spirit of Christ, and the other is built by men —carnal (Col 2:8, Rev 3:15-17), the counterfeit church, energized by the spirit of the anti-Christ.

CHAPTER 5

The Characteristics of the two Churches:

(It is recommended that all the scriptures are examined for personal or group study)

The Church built by Jesus.

1. It is invisible (Joh 4:23, Act 7:48, 17:24, 1Pet 2:5).
2. It consists only of the saved, those with personal encounter and relationship with Jesus (Act 2:47, 5:14) who gather in *ekklesia* to fellowship with one another (1Cor 14:26).
3. It is a local and autonomous gathering expressing the life of Christ without "branches" or "headquarters" (Eph 4:4-5, Rom 16:5, 1Cor 16:9).
4. Cannot be founded or headed by man, Christ is the head (1Cor 11:3, Eph 4:15, 5:35, Col 1:18).
5. It cannot be joined: membership is by birth only (Joh 3:3-5, Rom 8:29, Heb 12:23, 1Pe 1:23, 1Jn 5:18).
6. It is an organism, not an organization (Act 2:41, 5:14).

7. It is built on Jesus alone, not on doctrines, gifts, creeds, saints or man (1Cor 3:11, Mat 16:18).

8. It is not one man-led (Act 14:23, 15:2,4,22, 20:7, Eph 2:23, Col 1:18, 1Tim 5:17).

9. It has no building or physical structure (1Pet 2:5, Joh 4:21-24). The saints are the building blocks.

10. Leaders (elders) are brothers among the brethren, and servants, recognized by their calling (not titles, degrees, certificates, promotion, etc.) through the grace flowing through them to edify the body (Mat 20:25-28, Gal 5:13, 1Tim 5:12-13, Rom 12:6, 1Cor 4:6).

11. It is without human name (Rom 16:5, Col 4, 15, Phm 1:2, 1Cor 16:19, 1Tim 3:15).

12. Church meeting is not a one-man show or program but fellowship together with the saints (1Cor 14:26, Eph 4:11-14, 2Jn 1:7).

13. It owned by Lord Jesus, not by individual, organization, couple or family (Act 20:28, Eph 1:14).

14. Worship is in spirit and truth, and Spirit-led (Mat 26:30, Jon 4:23-24, Eph 5:19).

15. Love among brethren is supreme (Joh 13:34, Jon 15:12, 1Pet 4:8, Col 3:14 1Tim 1:5).

16. They preach Christ alone (Act 2:42, Heb 6:1, 2Jo 1:7).

17. It is Christ-centered, not crowd and multitude-driven (Mat 18:20, Act 2:42, Joh 6:26, 44, 1Cor 2:2).

18. No other attraction to lure people in except Golgotha and the cross (1Cor 2:2,4, Mat 8:34, Mar 10:21).

19. Giving is by the spirit and not by compulsion or coercing of the law. We give all of ourselves, not a part of us (Rom 12:8, 2Cor 8:12, 2:9:7, Phm 1:14, Luk 6:38, 2Cor 8:11-12, 9:7, Phi 3:19, 1Pet 4:10, Jud 11).

20. Preachers are ministers of righteousness in spirit and the gospel is deliverance from sin and eternal death (Mat 6:33, Eph 4:12, 2Cor 5:18).

The Church built by men:

1. It is visible. It has physical structures, altars, and officers (1Cor 3:16).

2. It consists of everyone, saved or unsaved who gather for religious service, programs, and to listen to a man or a select few.

3. It is an organization with head[quarter] / branches and common creed, laws, doctrines, etc.

4. It is founded and/or headed by man who is often the Overseer (1Cor 3:11).

5. It can be joined: membership is by choice, desire, interest or persuasion.

6. It is an organization. Some patterned along blue-chip, multi-national companies or corporations, with promotion, salary structure, etc.

7. It is built on doctrines, gifts, creeds, ideology, saints or men (1Cor 3:11, Mat 16:18).

8. It is one man (or few people) led and has visible head (1Cor 3:3-4).

9. It has buildings, properties, and physical structures referred to as "the Church" (1Pet 2:5, Joh 4:21-24).

10. Leaders are chief and special among the people and they have all authority. It is often by appointment, *secondment* or qualification. They are recognized by titles, degrees, costume, power

and influence (Mat 20:25-28, Mat 23:8-9).

11. It has human names, some reflecting names of the founder, saints or other choice names that identify it with a movement, group or sect.

12. Church meetings are often a program and a one man (or select few) show, not fellowship together with brethren. Members can only participate during tithe and offering time or other (Phi 3:18-19).

13. It is owned by individual, couple, family, organization, or movement, and they can solely appoint successor or inheritor.

14. Praise and Worship sessions are by paid "worship leaders" and instrumentalists who deliver rehearsed and professional session to simulate a spiritual mood or get people into sensual feelings (Mat 15:8).

15. Doctrine and performance is supreme (Phi 3, Gal 3, 5, Phi 2:2-9).

16. They preach and encourage the doctrine of Nicolaitans which Jesus said, "...which thing I hate" (Rev 2:6, 15), (Greek: Nikos = to subdue or dominate, Laos = people, i.e. clergy/laity control)

17. It is crowd and multitude-driven (Mat 18:20, Act 2:47, Joh 6:26, 66).

18. It has various pleasant attractions to lure people in and keep them coming (except Golgotha and

the cross) (2Tim 3:1-6, 2Tim 4:3,4).

19. Giving is by the law, compulsion and motivation (Mal 3:8-12, Heb 8:6-9, 2Cor 3:6)

20. Preachers are more of motivational speakers and minister to the soul. Their gospel is premised on the gains and benefits of the kingdom (Mat 6:33, 2Cor 2:17, 2Cor 11:4, 2Pet 2:1-3, Col 2:4, Rom 16:18).

It is clear that the foundation of the counterfeit church is anchored on a totally different experience to that of the true Church (Joh 4:23-34, 1Pet 2:5). This necessitates the presence of many religious centers carrying out creative and ingenious services with various attractions (music, breakthrough or financial seminars, miracles, etc) to bring crowd in.

The true Church is the gathering of those who are saved, otherwise, it is just a religious meeting place. "Then they that gladly received his word were baptized: and the same day there were added unto them about three thousand souls" (Act 2:41). "And believers were the more added to the Lord, multitudes both of men and women" (Act 5:14).

Christ graced some brothers within the gathering with leadership calling and ability to function (not as a title holders) in the "five-fold" ministry (Eph 4:11). They are to provide edification as they receive from Jesus who is the owner of His Church (1Cor 7:23). They are a channel to speak the truth in love that all "may grow up into him in all things, which is the head, even Christ: from whom the whole body fitly joined together and compacted by that which every joint supplieth, according to the effectual working in the measure of every part, maketh increase of the body unto the edifying of itself in love" (Eph 4:15-16).

Church Growth

As Satan's end approaches, he is racing against time to overrun the true Church of Jesus. He is not only enlarging his own church to accommodate the ever increasing and unsuspecting crowd, he is also moving fast to proliferate, reproduce and multiply everywhere.

> *Therefore hell hath enlarged herself, and opened her mouth without measure: and their glory, and their multitude, and their pomp, and he that rejoiceth, shall descend into it. (Isa 5:14)*

He is using pseudo-spiritual experiences, accommodative membership, bizarre and deregulated doctrines to lure many in. He is also using social appeal for a more viral growth among the youths calling it "church growth." He makes materialism, prosperity, and miracles evidences of God's approval and a sign of "success" in ministry. He seems to be winning especially among the so-called believers.

Church growth is not measured by these indices. It is neither a network of branches nor financial muscle for physical structures. Growth is not when we organize crowd-related programs in the name of evangelism. All these have the tendency to bring on the leaders the burden of performance, pleasing the people, and meeting their needs. Services are also likely to be flavored with activities and programs that appeal to the people and give a sense of fulfillment so as to keep them coming. While religious fulfillment is guaranteed, it will be ultimately challenging to experience personal relationship and the presence of Christ in such a place. (1Cor 2:4,13, 11:12)

Growth occurs in the gathering only when the Lord adds to His Church by Himself those that are saved (Act 2:47), not those we invite to our programs or special services.

Our responsibility as believers in fulfilling "The Great Commission" (Mar 16:15) is to GO OUT to where the sinners are and "disciple" (not merely convert) them. This means challenging them to face God with a message of true repentance to God and salvation in Christ (Act 2:38, 3:19, 8:22, 17:30, 26:20). All begins in God. If God does not "draw" a soul, he or she cannot come to Christ. Jesus said, "No man can come to me, except the Father which hath sent me draw him." (Joh 6:44)

We can make people recite the "sinners' prayer" and repent of their sins of lying, cheating, adultery, murder, etc, but that is hardly the repentance to salvation, it's at the best confession of sins, only meant for those who are saved and are already in Christ. The unsaved need repentance to God, which is to turn from death unto life; from left to right; from the lake of fire to heaven; from the camp of Satan to that of God, and not just to repent from the sins of cheating, and so on. This is the first step in the born again experience, and the message is sadly lacking in many pulpits today; it has been replaced with just "coming to Christ," and that God loves them so much and He's desperate to have them. God truly loves sinners and He has made provision for a sinner to come back to Him and that is the way of repentance. "The times of this ignorance God winked at; but now commandeth all men every where to repent." (Act 17:30)

When a born again believer commits a sin (lying, cheating, etc), that does not make him a "sinner" because "whosoever is born of God doth not commit sin; for his seed remaineth in him: and he cannot sin, because he is born of God" (1Joh 3:9). He just "fell" into sin and if he asks for forgiveness from the heart, he will be forgiven (1Joh 2:1). But a soul that is yet to repent from "dead works" (Heb 6:1) cannot ask for forgiveness because "God heareth not sinners" (Joh 9:31). He did not fall into sin, he is living in it; it is a lifestyle to him. He needs to first realize this and turn to God first. This is called "godly sorrow."

For godly sorrow worketh repentance to salvation not to be repented of: but the sorrow of the world worketh death. (2Cor 7:10)

This is not to be sorry for being stupid enough to be caught for a sin, or to regret one's haplessness, but it's a genuine sorrow for being alienated from Father God, i.e. not knowing God, and being on the way to the lake of fire. This realization gives birth to the sorrow of heart and an inner longing for a way back to God. But then, he discovers that there is a gulf that separates him and God, and he needs someone to take him through. This is when the need for that someone (savior) dawns.

At this juncture, many souls give in to "pressures" from those who claim to be the savior but are not. Some follow a system, movement or religion thinking it can bridge the gulf and lead them to God. But when the soul is patient and wait on God to lead to the right Savior, God leads to His Son. God does not lead to any religion, not even Christianity. This is when the light of the glorious gospel shines and he sees that Christ is the only qualified Mediator and Advocate between God and man (1Tim 2:5). He is the only One who can take man across the gulf and to God. (2Cor 4:4)

It is the Father that leads to Christ after a "godly sorrow," and when such comes to Christ, Christ will hold them to the end. (Joh 17:12) Jesus said,

All that the Father giveth me shall come to me; ...of all which he hath given me I should lose nothing, but should raise it up again at the last day. (Joh 6:37, 39)

It is challenging for anyone who has not experienced an initial encounter with God (Godly sorrow) through repentance to come to Christ. This is why many end up in religion, even Christian religion and not Christ. Our message to the lost is to repent of the original sin of alienation from God, lifestyle of sin and religion, and turn 180 degrees to God and He will save them by leading them to His Son (the Savior) who will bring them to Him.

We cannot bypass God in the presentation of the Gospel of salvation to people. We cannot simply ask them to believe and come to Christ without the initial repentance to God. To believe and come to Christ is right but it is after godly sorrow when they realize the need for a savior. This is why a lot of people profess Christ but are still ungodly in character.

There is a lot of Christianity around the world but less godliness. There are many so-called believers and even leaders but with questionable character let alone righteousness. "By their fruits you will know them." How can we speak and demonstrate so much of Christ and our lives is not Christ-like. Whatever does not begin in God cannot return to Him. Our coming back to God must be initiated by Him, and He has done that by giving Christ. Jesus always says He can do nothing of Himself but what He sees the Father do (Joh 5:19).

The Father will only draw when people turn to Him in repentance. And when the Father draws such a soul to Christ, Christ places them in His Church because that is the only thing He is building and coming back for.

The Church is the 'family house:' a place where Christ nurtures, builds, trains, and prepares His bride for His return. There cannot be proper discipleship outside the Church setting because that is the only place all nourishments and functionings are provisioned. It is the symbol of Christ's authority on earth, which believers must be under and demonstrate through expression in a local gathering. This is the place of Christ-centered discipleship involving not only one "discipler" but all ministry giftings and graces functioning together to edify. It is just like in a family setting where we have parents and siblings all contributing to the growth of each other, yet recognizing everyone's unique place and grace, particularly the "parents" as "disciplers." (1Cor 4:15) This is where and how we can have all the fullness of the Godhead bodily and we will be complete in Him (Col 2:9). That is the function of the Church.

A local gathering is when and where two or three believers gather to express the life in and of Christ, and Jesus (not prayer, music, doctrine, message, etc) is the object, subject, and attraction of the gathering (Mat

18:20). The early Church met in houses providing a pattern for us (1Cor 1:11, 1Cor 16:19). Such gathering is a place where we can be ourselves without the formality of being religious. We can freely express ourselves in fellowship, ask questions, contribute and really know ourselves. We will know those who are weak and those who have graces in certain ministries and we can all be edified. This is when there can be an abiding in Him, growing from in to out, and then we can abound in Him, bearing fruits (Joh 15).

CHAPTER 6
The Kingdom and the Glory

Be sober, be vigilant; your adversary the devil,
as a roaring lion, walketh about, seeking whom
he may devour: Whom resist stedfast in the
faith, knowing that the same afflictions
are accomplished in your brethren
that are in the world. (1Pet 5:8)

SATAN IS A serial deceiver... he deceived the first bride (Eve) and she died a spiritual death (Gen 3:4). He is not relenting with the second bride, the Church. He hates her because He knows she has the key to his end.

Satan took Jesus to the highest mountain and showed him all "the kingdoms of the world and the glory of them." He said to Him:

All these things will I give thee, if thou wilt fall
down and worship me. (Mat 4:9)

His silver and gold are default blessings to his counterfeit bride, but he must lure the virgin bride into it. He is more generous with his gifts at this end time than he had ever been. Maybe he had first tried to deceive Adam in the Garden and failed before he found an in-road with Eve. He succeeded with her anyway:

And when the woman saw that the tree was good for food, and that it was pleasant to the eyes, and a tree to be desired to make one wise, she took of the fruit thereof, and did eat, and gave also unto her husband with her; and he did eat. (Gen 3:6)

He also tried Jesus in the wilderness and he failed. Now he is going after the true Church. He feels that since he succeeded with the bride of the first Adam, he could succeed with the bride of the second Adam. But Jesus Christ defeated him with "it is written." Let not it be far away from your mouth:

And they overcame him by the blood of the Lamb, and by the word of their testimony; and they loved not their lives unto the death. (Rev 12:11)

Eve was brought down by deception. Satan posed the same deception to Jesus in the wilderness and he is also offering the same to the bride of Christ, the

Church. He is offering the "whole world" to the Church. He is offering the gift of the kingdom and the glory of the kingdom to the Church; fame, wealth, popularity, power, and even special gifts. Just like Eve saw Satan's gifts as good for food, pleasant to the eyes and make one wise. Now the church also says:

I am rich, and increased with goods, and have need of nothing; and knowest not that thou art wretched, and miserable, and poor, and blind, and naked. (Rev 3:17)

This is the Laodecian Church, the church that Satan built himself, the counterfeit bride. Jesus says to her:

I counsel thee to buy of me gold tried in the fire, that thou mayest be rich; and white raiment, that thou mayest be clothed, and that the shame of thy nakedness do not appear; and anoint thine eyes with eyesalve, that thou mayest see. As many as I love, I rebuke and chasten: be zealous therefore, and repent. (Rev 3:18-19)

But that is just a counsel. Will she adhere to it? Jesus cannot be frustrated by the Laodecian Church's decision or choice. He is irrevocably committed to His promise to build His Church: a bride without spot, stain, wrinkle or blemish. A bride that will be presentable to the Father and would defeat the adversary. He is still on course, regardless of the choice of the Laodecian Church.

Look around, you will see the glory, riches, and wealth of the Laodecian [counterfeit] Church and her "ministers." She has everything. She has bowed to Satan in secret and demonstrating the glory in the public. The glory and power that looks so close to the original so much that the "very elect" can be deceived. The miracles, signs, and wonders are the generosity of Satan in order to have followership, mega-congregation, mighty cathedrals, empires, institutions, positions, and even cities. This is real and all around us today, the church that Satan built and blessed. He has his own ministers who transform as "angel of lights." They control the world. He told Jesus: "all these things I will give to you." If he would risk giving it to Jesus, he would lavish it on his own to achieve his aim.

Among his ministers are sincere men and women who have simply and sincerely believed a lie like Eve did. They are in the fore-front of dressing sin rather than addressing it, and also giving it an alternative and fanciful name. They would rather offend God than offend people. They emphasize hyper-grace and other "exemption clauses." They change the definition of the Church from people to building, make leading brothers in the gathering officers, brought money into the Church, turn ministry to what we can give to God and call salvation what we offer to Him, and so on.

Remember, the counterfeit bride is called, "the great whore that sitteth upon many waters;" she has the people and controls the populace. She makes them drunk with her "wine" (sweet doctrines, music, and other appeals). It should not be difficult to see a semblance of this around. Remember also, that she is "arrayed in purple and scarlet colour, and decked with gold and precious stones and pearls, having a golden cup in her hand."

The counterfeit church has gained many grounds, people, power, and control so much that it looks futile to fight it. It is a monster and an institution that cannot be fought. It's only logical to either flow with the tide or follow a wise instruction:

Come out from among them, and be ye separate, saith the Lord, and touch not the unclean thing; and I will receive you, And will be a Father unto you, and ye shall be my sons and daughters, saith the Lord Almighty. (2Cor 6:17- 18)

All disobedience will be rebuked when our obedience is complete (2Cor 10:6). Jesus is waiting to receive as many as will run as fast as their legs can carry them out of the organized religious system of the counterfeit church, and receive them into His fold. So that there will be one fold and one shepherd (Joh 10:16).

Christ is busy preparing His bride [the remnants] that will not bow to this gigantic organized religious system of a beautiful but counterfeit bride who is in control of the destiny of billions of sincere people who desire to worship God but end up worshipping the mystery woman, the abominations of the earth.

Final Words

A S IT IS written, the slave woman (the counterfeit church) cannot hinder or inherit The Promise (Gen 21:10-12, Rom 9:7, Heb 11:18). She cannot overcome the true Church, and the gate of hell cannot prevail against the Church of the living God. The word of Christ is still potent and true, and it should comfort us: "…I will build my Church…" (Mat 16:18).

Although Adam fell to the adversary in the Garden of Eden, but Jesus overcame him in the Garden of Gethsemane. He has given us power and authority to do the same (Luk 10:17-19, Mar 16:17-18, 1Cor 15:8).

Satan failed with the first Church (God redeemed her), he failed with the early Church (God preserved her), he will also fail with the remnant Church (God will rescue her). Let the remnant be comforted with this truth also (Heb 13:10).

The remnant Church is the prophetic re-presentation of the Philadelphia Church, the rapturable and rapture-ready Church (Rev 3:8-13). She is undenominated, uncontaminated and has not defiled herself with the king's delicacies. She is not built, led, headed or founded by man... To be a part is to be born (again) of water and of spirit (spiritual birth). When these gather in twos or threes or more, and wherever that may be to express Christ only (not their needs or idea of worship) in spirit and in truth, Jesus is there as the Head. That is the expression of the true Church (Mat 18:20, Joh 4:21-24). Brethren without class, caste, hierarchy or clergy-laity divide (Gal 3:28, Col 3:11), but simply recognizing different graces among themselves for proper functioning and edification of the whole body "...till we all come in the unity of the faith..." (Eph 4:12).

The hour cometh, and now is, when the true worshippers shall worship the Father in spirit and in truth: for the Father seeketh such to worship him. God is a Spirit: and they that worship him must worship him in spirit and in truth. (Joh 4:23-24)

Let us rejoice in the "blessed hope" that Jesus will preserve His bride from the strange woman, the counterfeit church with all her allure, grandeur, and persecution (Tit 2:13, 2The 2:16, Eph 5:6, Rev 3:10). He will also keep us from the "Wicked One" and the "evil day" unto His glorious appearing (1Joh 2:14, 5:18). Even so, come, Lord Jesus!

He that hath an ear, let him hear what the Spirit saith unto the churches; To him that overcometh will I give to eat of the hidden manna, and will give him a white stone, and in the stone a new name written, which no man knoweth saving he that receiveth it. (Rev 2:17)

And the Spirit and the bride say, Come. And let him that heareth say, Come. And let him that is athirst come. And whosoever will, let him take the water of life freely. (Rev 22:17)

≈ ≈ ≈

OTHER BOOKS BY THE AUTHOR

- What God Forgot To Say
- Mystery of Union in Marriage
- Capsules of Faith

UPCOMING BOOKS

- The Companion Booklet to The Normal Christian Cycle
- Spiritual Recipe: Five Ingredients of a Godly Marriage

You may contact the author for
comments, questions, or other inquiries:

✉ E-mail: olujordan@gmail.com
Facebook: bolaolujordan
Twitter: ojordanist

The GreatPossession

Riches and Wealth are Great Possessions, But There is a Greater Possession...

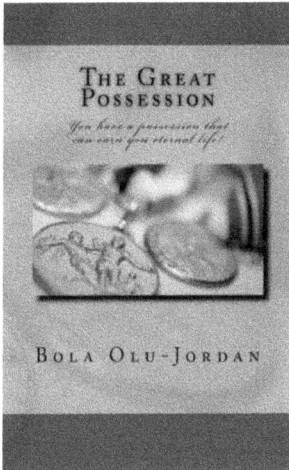

Author: Bola Olu-Jordan
Format: Paperback/Kindle
Pages: 73 Pages Paperback
ISBN: 978978-5037715
Publisher: CRYOUT Publishing

Available on Amazon

When do riches, wealth or possessions become stumbling block to get to the kingdom of God and when do they become asset leading to the Kingdom? This book will help you discover this and how the most difficult things you could ever let go in your life can be a blessing, rather than a spiritual burden in your Christian journey.

～～～

I Know Your Works

Your eternity depends on the verdict of one Man and He has something against you!

Author: Bola Olu-Jordan
Format: Paperback / Kindle
Pages: 84, Paperback
ISBN: 978-9785037739
Publisher: CRYOUT Publishing

Available on Amazon

You are invited to the banquet of a Great King by one of His lords. You bring your best gift to honor the king. He likes the gift, but your name is not in the guest list. Only the prince can bring you in, but he wants something you don't have. When your works and labor are acceptable to God, what else could He be looking for? This book shows you what it is, and how you can have it. It is the only requirement to make heaven!

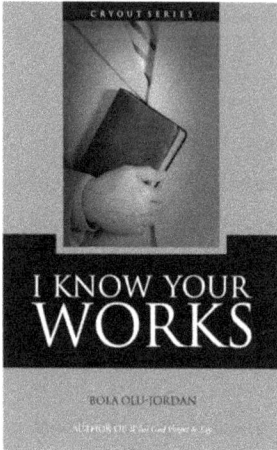

∽ ∽ ∽

The Normal Christian Cycle:
Unlocking the Secret to the Fullness of Christ

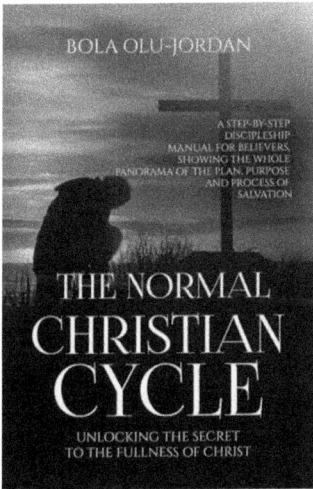

Author: Bola Olu-Jordan
Format: Paperback / Kindle
Pages: 256 pages, paperback
ISBN: 9785037746
Publisher: CRYOUT Publishing

Available on Amazon

**IMAGINE IF WINTER WERE
THE ONLY SEASON!**

**You would never know the beauty of the other
seasons when your choice was based only on the
experience of one.**

God wants you to experience all, not just a part of
Him. The church has lost four fundamental principles
and secrets necessary for believers to experience the
fullness of Christ. This book reveals what they are and
how you can get them.

~ ~ ~

About The Author

Bola Olu-Jordan grew up in Africa where much of his spiritual development was birthed. He pastored in a large denomination for several years and was actively involved in church planting, mission outreaches, discipleship and leadership trainings. He presently fellowships with a local gathering from where the Lord open doors of fellowship with brethren around the world. He is married and blessed with children.

NOTES